G000231633

HOME PORT

AN OUTLINE OF
SHIPPING ACTIVITIES
IN WHITBY FROM MONASTIC
TIMES TO THE 1980's

by

ALFRED LUND

Printed by Maxiprint, Designers and Colour Printers, York
Telephone (0904) 692000

Whitby Harbour Entrance
by *John Freeman (Whitby Artist)*

FOREWORD

There have been many publications dealing with aspects of Whitby's history - probably the two best known locally being the works of Lionel Charlton (1779) and the Rev, George Young (1817). P. Shaw Jeffrey M.A. F.R.G.S. (1952) was one of the latest to attempt a generalised account in his *Whitby Lore and Legend*; but he dealt mainly with personalities and legends and his descriptions of industries and the people involved, which were the life-blood of the town, were commented on only briefly. I found it almost incredible that the fishing industry was hardly mentioned.

There is an obvious necessity to refer to the important influence of the monastery on Whitby and its people or the part of the Cholmleys in local affairs but I consider also, that in 1992 we should evaluate the ordinary 'run of the mill' history that involved the town's folk just as much, or even more so, than some of the famous names mentioned, although considerable that their activities undoubtedly were.

I, personally, found Robert Tate Gaskin's account of *The Old Seaport of Whitby* (1908) very readable when compared with some of the scholarly histories subscribed by some former writers.

They were, however, writing for an educated minority and not for general consumption. As education did not become compulsory until the late 19th century it is fairly accurate to state that there were still quite large numbers of people who were illiterate and so unable to understand the academic reasonings of erudite historians.

I have attempted to write an outline of what, one might consider, was the most important factor in the life of the town, that of shipping in practically all its aspects. I have not included the Royal Navy in which many local men served, or made it their careers, but take it for granted that such recognition is universal throughout the country.

It is a brief outline so I make no claim to its originality or to compare it with former academic approaches other than to remark that I have tried to include some factors that may be as much of a surprise to some as they were to me.

Nearly everyone becomes nostalgic when 'looking back' especially when old photos or paintings recall memories more vividly. Some of the pictorial additions are artists' impressions and the frontispiece is a sufficiently impressive and relative work of art, depicting a vessel returning to its home port.

The Sutcliffe photographs are a valuable aid to the contents of this booklet and I was fortunate in securing other photographs relevant to the account.

Footnote: - It is sad to relate that both Gaskin and Shaw Jeffrey never lived to see their quite valuable works published.

MAP OF WHITBY 1778

HOME PORT

Everyone, I hope, has a 'home port' either in the literal or the metaphorical sense and the home port of Whitby has meant much to many people, particularly those who trace their ancestry back centuries. So why the great attraction? - it's an indefinable one I have to state - not only is it a picturesque place of beauty on a bleak and savage coastline but owing to its religious connections of bygone times it became well known in many far off places so that most habitations, even great cities of today, cannot compare. It has a timeless appeal, superficial changes have taken place but essentially the town remains the same.

There were several factors which contributed to Whitby's development as a port. Firstly and most obviously, was its fortunate geographical location and also with a river mouth which provided harbour refuge, the best between the Tees and the Humber.

In centuries long gone by the area had been visited by many ships, the Roman galleys, the clumsy but serviceable craft of the Saxon pirates and later again the terrifying, long ships of the Vikings, which from a technical point of view were much advanced on the aforementioned vessels.

Without doubt the Vikings eventually settled in the district around, the name Whitby is derived from the Scandinavian language, and they brought with them their knowledge of ship construction. This skill was utilized by them to improve the existing boats built by the Saxon people who settled here. This in turn could have led to the construction of the typical coble which became such a feature in later shipbuilding.

The monastic establishment on the East Cliff, both in Saxon and Norman times was responsible however, for influencing the use of the river mouth as a recognised harbour. The religious significance of the monastery became widely known and visits to and from the abbey, established its importance in the two periods mentioned above.

THE MONASTERY OF WHITBY

Since the monastery and its abbey had been refounded by the Normans in the 11th century, the town's folk in general had come to depend on the employment, readily available to satisfy the monastic requirements. Many worked as labourers on the land or on the various buildings, but the fisherfolks' ability to supply plenty of fish required by the brethren within the monastery, to comply with religious observances, had led to the growth of a substantial fishing industry, relatively speaking.

The monastic authorities were usually able to dispose of surplus fish supplies (collected by way of tithes) to foreign ships which entered the river mouth bringing goods which they bartered for fish. This trade made the monastery richer, even if it offered little recompense for the fishermen.

The fishing cobles at this time were built by the fishermen themselves who constructed them to their individual needs but conforming, more or less, to the traditional type of craft considered by them to be a sea-worthy vessel.

All fishing was of the inshore type, the men being only too familiar with the inhospitable coast line and its many hazards.

Furthermore, it is correct to state that at the time under discussion most boats were propelled by oar power, the addition of a sail being a rarity owing to the expense (canvas, ropes, tackle etc).

This long era of employment provided by the monastery came to an abrupt finish when the Dissolution of the Monasteries was implemented (in Whitby - 1539). Townsfolk were immediately aware of the loss of livelihood they then suffered and had to endure many decades of hardship before the development of the alum industry once again brought employment to the town, particularly in the labouring field.

ALUM AND TRANSPORTATION REQUIREMENTS

Whitby's subsequent growth was due to the discovery of alum in the locality in the late 16th century. This find leading to the need for a number of simple industrial processes to extract and purify the raw material, grey alum shale, used in the new industry in order to obtain the alum crystals. These processes, necessitating, both from sources near or far, other raw materials which required a considerable use of transport facilities. Coal was needed from the coal ports of Durham and Northumberland and eventually the despatching of tons of alum crystals to various places throughout Britain and the Continent.

Land transport was impossible in those days for the carriage of large mass quantities of materials and the obvious method was to use sea or river transport if the latter was available and satisfactory.

Fisherfolk were quick to see the conveyance of raw materials could prove a source of income - meagre though it was and so this demand was at first satisfied by the fishing community many of whom badly needed the work. They welcomed the opportunity of employment they could undertake with their cobles as the work afforded by the monastery had ceased some decades previously.

Yet another transport consideration was the conveyance of quantities of human urine (uric acid) to be used in the refining process. This was at first collected locally but later with the growth of the industry greater quantities were required which meant obtaining it from areas with a greater population - London being the main source. The urine was conveyed in casks and neither the skippers nor their boats were given much respect. It was said that the strongest word of contempt at that time was to refer to a mariner as being the master of such a craft. The 'aroma' that was emitted from the vessels, casks and tackle generally, was said to be considerable and unpleasant.

It is recorded that some fishermen joined together to purchase two or three vessels (probably sloops) which were more suitable and would more easily make the longer passages to Sunderland, Newcastle, London or elsewhere with the finished product. There were numerous sloops (colliers), a little bigger than cobles, carrying coal to various towns and villages along the coast or rivers long before the alum industry was established, so it is not improbable that a similar type of vessel was constructed by Whitby fishermen to satisfy the demand that now arose. Sloops were between 35 and 50 tons and could carry 50 tons of coal.

The local coble, having the reputation of a well-built sea craft, was used as a prototype to build vessels with similar features which would fulfil the requirements of the industry. There was plenty of good oak to be had locally for the construction of masts, yards, bowsprits, a mixture of oak and pine too for decks, whilst Helmsley elm was also used for the keels, the wood being known for its water resisting qualities. There were no named ship-yards in Whitby at that time (late 16th century) so as yet the ship construction business was in its infancy. Nevertheless, the provision of ships for the fetching and carrying of coal, seaweed,

Unloading coal at Sandsend. The usual method of unloading bulk cargoes before the use of steam power and when no port facilities were available. (Sutcliffe Gallery)

urine and so on for the alum workings brought a new activity into the port and renewed commercial interest into a town which was soon to establish a new enterprise - that of skilled ship construction.

THE INNER AND OUTER HARBOURS

It is obvious when dealing with ship-building one takes it for granted that port facilities are there or being developed. Of relative interest then are the comments of Charlton and Young (local historians) regarding the existence of at least one pier in place long before the closure of the monastery. In Henry VIII's reign, John Leland, (circa 1530) writer and antiquarian wrote of a pier or piers he had seen when visiting Whitby and too, there are records of bequests made by two local men in their wills which mention sums of money to be used in pier and harbour maintenance. An earlier record in the reign of Edward I states that the king made a grant for the upkeep of a quay 'newly constructed' at Whitby (March 1307). He also sanctioned that 'harbour dues' could be collected for a period in aid of this construction. There is not a clear indication as to whether the 'quay' was the pier to which he referred. However, these comments and conclusions by Charlton and Young point to the fact that Whitby had a well used harbour long before the alum industry injected new life into the area.

Whitby lower harbour - in the latter part of 19th century.

The port was the recipient of various royal grants to be used in the repair of the quay or quays, but the references are somewhat ambiguous as there are allusions to the quay being 'decayed and broken down by the force of the sea' on more than one occasion. If by 'quay' a wharf was meant, one may ask - in what position was a wharf to be so broken down by the sea? A conclusion might be drawn that, in fact it was the pier to which the references were made.

In 1632 a collection was instigated by Sir Hugh Cholmley for the 're-edifying of the piers'. In the Cholmley memoirs, Sir Hugh states that 'part of the pier to the west of the harbour was rebuilt and by doing so preserved a great part of the town from being ruined by the sea' which is easy to imagine when a real Northerly wind blows.

This century (20th) the storm of 1953 was the worst in living memory - a large part of England was almost devastated along the eastern coasts. In Whitby all the piers were awash *(see the late Mr. Winks letter page 9)*, so too was Church Street, New Quay Road and the Dock End Car Park. At one point it was reported that boats were floating around where cars should have been - there should be someone still around who could verify that story. It does not need much imagination to realize that in former times the conditions would have been much worse if such a storm hit the town and the reference to the possible ruination of half the town was no exaggeration.

The protection of the pier seemed to have been failing even before the sea trade with the monastery ended. Reports state the harbour channel was frequently blocked by sand and rocks washed in from the west. The pier was often broken down by the fury of the storms and there was always the sediment and debris washed down by the river to contend with.

In the early part of the 18th century a concerted effort was made to improve port facilities for the benefit of the growing trade. A petition was sent to Parliament requiring that money be made available to re-build and maintain the piers.

To be brief, the money was found. Gaskin states that the East Pier was built early in the 18th century and the West Pier was strengthened and lengthened from time to time; but - he had remarked previously, that the money raised 'enabled the Trustees to *complete* the building of the piers which formed the lower harbour.' Suppositions

When only the lighthouse tops were visible . . .

are not necessarily helpful but as there are several references to the two main piers one can only assume they were in place even if in the form of 'glorified breakwaters'. Dr. Young's statement that the small inner pier known as Tatehill Pier seemed to have been formed out of the original East Pier leads one to think that Gaskin meant that the East Pier was re-built at the time indicated. The West Pier lighthouse was built with Aislaby stone in 1831 and the one on the East Pier in 1854.

The entering of the port is difficult in bad weather and despite the addition of the two extensions in 1914, continues to be a hazardous manoeuvre requiring skilful handling from the skipper of any boat endeavouring to do so. How much more difficult it was in former days is realized when references state it was the usual practice for many ships to avoid a winter passage. Nearly all the alum boats were open (no deck) even though many were now supplied with sail and to manoeuvre such vessels was an acquired skill even in fair weather. My own opinion is that the reference must have been a generalization as I cannot visualise Whitby fishermen confined to port in 'fear' of a potential bad weather threat unless they had reason to think a storm was imminent.

There were other dangers to be reckoned with as well as the winter gales. Attacks by privateers (French or Dutch) and at times by pirates, or even the unwelcome attention of the Press Gang could lose ships, deplete crews, and endanger projects.

Judging by ships' accounts researched by Gaskin it is obvious that Whitby's development in ship-construction was accelerated by the demands made by the alum

Rough Sea off Whitby

Whitby - A Rough Night

industry. In such accounts references are made to ship-wrights, sail-makers, rope makers and so on. The names of three ships built early in the 17th century indicates that by that time, there appears to have been at least one working yard plus the fact that there were at that time craftsmen who had either come to Whitby or had been trained here. These details lead one to the conclusion that the demand for ships had certainly encouraged craftsmen to migrate to our old town at some point. It is clear too, that successful building of craft for the alum trade was also earning a good reputation for the port as a ship building centre. Merchandise (other than alum) brought and taken from the expanding port was creating scope for the construction of various types of ships for which there was a need.

Having made that statement, it appears, after reading Rosalin Barker's paper in a recent Whitby Literary & Philosophical Society's publication, that the discussion of the development of local ship-building was more complex than I have stated. She has discovered through research that in the mid-1620's a ship, the 'Great Neptune' (500 tons) built by Andrew Dickson, was in fact constructed at Whitby, and so destroys the assumption that ship tonnage was limited to around 200 tons.

My remark that there must have been a working yard seems to have now been justified as the sources quoted by Mrs. Barker are reliable. Whether the 'Great Neptune' was built on temporary stocks or in an established yard is not recorded.

WHITBY GAZETTE
Saturday, 17 March, 1883

Another Storm — High Tide: After a few hours of comparative calm, the weather in this locality again became very severe on Sunday last. The wind blew with great force, there was an extraordinarily high tide in the evening, which swept the whole of the piers, while many of the tenements in Baxtergate and Church Street, and on the dock end, were flooded, causing great inconvenience to the occupiers. Church Street was impassable from the Hospitals downwards.

Snow has fallen every day since, and work on the Scarboro' line has been almost stopped, while outdoor labour generally is greatly impeded. The heavy sea on the coast washed up the wreck of the Elizabeth Austen, which drove on shore on the 28th October, 1880, and had been lifted out of the sand on Saturday last, under the direction of the harbour master.

The remains of the Star of Hope, which had drifted to sea, was washed into the harbour on Monday.

* * *

EARLY SHIP BUILDING

The three ships mentioned above were named the 'Pelican' (170 tons), the Margaret (110 tons), and 'Love's Increase' (110 tons) and the fact that they were Whitby built is verified by a reference to Trinity House whose certificates show they were allowed to carry defensive ordnances (guns). These certificates were granted in 1626 & 1627 and establishes definitely that ships other than cobles and sloops were being constructed at Whitby. A reference was made on the certificate that each one was Whitby built. Ship construction then was carried on successfully, quite early in the 17th century, obviously by improved methods of construction which were well known locally.

Regarding harbour facilities it was clear that the inner harbour (above the old bridge) was a sheltered area with potential ship-yard sites on either the East or West bank of the Esk. (See map). It was on the West Bank that the first named ship-yard developed on or near the site of the present railway station. This event took place at

This is how the Dock End looked at high tide, right up to the Early Thirties when it was filled in and made into a car-park. The painting must have been done in the latter part of the 19th century as it can be seen St. Michael's Church had been built.

the end of the 17th century, Jarvis Coates being the owner and ship-builder. Of relative interest many may recall that up till the mid 20th century there was a low mud bank exposed at low tide in the middle of the inner harbour, known as Bell Island - where the Marina now stands. It was the custom in the days of sail, to moor a ship there with a broom lashed to its masthead - as a sign that it was up for sale.

Abraham's Bosom was the stretch of river shore where the Penny Hedge is planted and it was there the whalers beached their ships for scraping and cleaning barnacles and weed from the keel and hull when necessary. There was no Church Street, at that point, in those times - at low tide one could walk under the ornate figure heads on the bows. It was no wonder that Whitby was able to augment its growing ship building industry as such natural facilities were available.

The thriving alum trade had fed the demand for ships to be built and as early as 1730 Custom accounts show that ninety vessels entered the port with general cargoes, an indication that the harbour trade was flourishing. In 1733 307 vessels arrived with coal, some boats were small (5 men to each boat as in Monastic times).

Trade from the port was varied with a considerable amount of local produce such as butter and eggs (of which there was a surfeit locally), flour from Ruswarp Mill, tallow candles, made by William Storm of Sandsend, hams, beeswax, pickled fish and potted lobster, all destined for London. It should be remembered at that time that sea transport was the most convenient method to convey surplus farm or fish produce to an ever demanding capital city as well as to Hull, Stockton, Newcastle and various other ports on the coast.

Middlesbrough was not in existence in those times. Regarding Ruswarp Mill I recall, in the late 20's, a small half-choked channel running from the town side of the

12

RIVER TEES, STOCKTON   Nº 615.

Stockton about the mid 19th century - an important market for produce from Whitby and district as detailed in text. There are two small tugs, otherwise it is still the days of sail.

Mill and connecting with the river. It could have provided access for a small boat to load flour and transport it down to Whitby. In fact I remember on occasions a couple of small boats, one with a mast, moored at the mouth of this inlet, behind the Bridge Inn. According to records this channel was the lower part of the weir carrying the water at the side of the mill and thus driving the water wheel. In 1912 an improvement was made whereby the old paddle wheel type was modified. The direction of the millrace was altered to go straight under the mill and into the river, the new wheel being built into the addition constructed at the west end of the mill after a fire in 1911. Whether or not the disused channel was used for transport is not recorded. There was however, a wharf on the river side of the mill so that was probably sufficient.

None of this growing trade would have developed without increased ship-building and particularly in the late 18th century the demand for ships grew, a number of yards being opened to supply the demand. Orders were coming in for vessels which were known to be strong, reliable and cheap and ports such as London, Liverpool, Shields and Hull were placing the orders. Greenock also ordered a number of large ships for their trade with the West Indies.

WHALING INDUSTRY

There was yet another factor to be considered in Whitby's role as a ship-building port - this was the Whaling Industry which commenced in 1735. The government of the day was giving a bounty on whale oil and discerning shipowners and merchants with an eye on the handsome profits that could be made were eager to either finance such a venture or themselves sail up to the seas around Greenland where the whales were to be caught.

13

For the whaling trade, very strong ships were required to withstand the constant danger of being crushed by pack ice. Whitby yards rose to the demands of the whalers for stronger bows which were doubled or even trebled to overcome the abnormal ice pressures they encountered.

CONDITIONS

A relevant fact that sheds light on conditions in sailing ships is the large number of crew who were needed, in relation to the tonnage and size of the vessel. Sails had to be hoisted, adjusted to half sail, lowered or on occasions tied back to the yards in storm periods to avoid being torn to shreds. To heave up the anchor on the capstan needed six to eight men and there was always a man up in the crow's nest watching out for a sighting of their quarry. A statement was made when a remark was made about the fo'c'sle's crowded condition that the men were quite used to such, as the yards and alleys (a characteristic feature of Whitby and the fishing villages adjacent) in which they lived whilst at home were just as crowded and devoid of much sunshine. This comparison is of interest but as far as the crews were concerned the work afforded a livelihood perilous though it might have been.

Despite the hazardous conditions of ice, treacherous weather conditions and attendant dangers it is recorded that only 13 whalers were lost, in that period, out of a fleet of fifty three. One of the thirteen, the 'Nautilus,' was burnt down to the keel in Whitby when almost ready to sail for the Arctic. Another the 'Phoenix' nearly made the count up to fourteen when, during a savage gale she was driven into the side of an iceberg with such force that the crew almost gave up hope. She cleared the 'berg' however, and by good luck and good management made it back to her home port of Whitby. An almost 'comic' finale occurred when the crew were hurriedly recalled, from either pubs or church on the Sunday, the day after arrival, to help pump out the ship which was sinking at her moorings. She did meet her end at Whitby as will be described below.

A reminder of the dangers faced by the seamen engaged in this tough, brutal trade when retold sound almost incredible as the hardships and sufferings which befell them were too numerous to relate. One of the many disasters for a whaler was to be nipped by the ice and compelled to remain ice-locked for an Artic winter; quite frequently running out of fuel, food and water, with temperatures both inside and outside the ship so low as to make one wonder that any man survived at all - whaling ships were sometimes lost without trace. In one sense, if they came through such an experience, they were lucky despite the frost-bitten areas of their bodies, some losing toes, fingers, ears, some of which they broke off themselves or were cut off by the ship's surgeon! With some, gangrene set in and death resulted long before they saw their home port. At times ships were crushed beyond repair and their luckless crews took to the ice-floes inevitably to perish unless by pure chance another whaler was in a position to rescue them. Other ships were forced up on to the floes by the pressure of the ice and lay on their sides until milder weather allowed them to slip back into an open 'run' of water with the depleted and weakened crew members doing what they could to hoist the sails and head south. Shetland and Orkney men were often crew members as it was the custom for outward bound whaling ships to stop at either Kirkwall or Lerwick to take on fresh supplies and allow the crew a final fling ashore. If they required any men to complete a crew there were always island men ready to take their chance and hopefully share in the bounty provided by a good season.

WHALING SHIPS

Whale ships were, on average, between 200 & 300 tonnage. Square rigged and built as robustly as possible - they sacrificed speed for strength.

The Eclipse, a whale ship from Aberdeen, once an important whaling port.

This whaling-ship has been built with a type of marine steam engine but clearly relies on sail as a reliable method of propulsion.

CHAPEL STREET
ROBIN HOODS BAY

ARGUMENTS YARD.

Two of the old yards referred to when discussing living conditions on the whale ships and 'similar' conditions back home.

ARGUMENTS YARD Whitby is still very much the same; Ulric Walmsley's CHAPEL STREET looks very picturesque and neither...

16

We tend to forget this particular era of seamanship where men struggled to bring back a commodity which brought comfort and convenience to the folk back home but for which hundreds paid with their lives. Mark Adler's book 'The Greenlander' tells a fascinating if grim story of this not so distant period.

The accounts of the Scoresbys describe vividly the conditions encountered when whaling and without doubt the reputation of Whitby vessels, generally withstanding such experiences, was greatly enhanced as tales of the severity of the weather and conditions became widely known.

CAPTAIN COOK

Nowadays commercial interests of one sort or another regard publicity as a valuable aid to the businesses they are trying to manage for their best interests. It is in this context that I recall the fame of Captain Cook in regard to his influence in spreading knowledge of Whitby's boat-building prowess. He certainly had the experience of them even down to serving his apprenticeship in a collier brig, the 'Freelove', making numerous passages on the East coast like so many other crew members of hundreds of similar vessels. To say he was instrumental in promoting yet more interest in Whitby-built craft is certainly correct but his reasons were more practical than for any reason of publicity. Much has been written of his exploits so I will refrain from any further comments.

The demand for Whitby ships grew - Cook's voyages were made at the same time the whaling industry was in full spate so if one wonders why the importance of local shipping was so extensive these two facts alone explain.

FURTHER SHIP-CONSTRUCTION DEVELOPMENTS

In the second half of the 18th century and the first half of the 19th, a number of ship-yards situated around the inner harbour prospered, turning out a variety of vessels. Names like the Barrys, Barricks, Brodericks, Campions, Fishburns, Langbournes had yards on either side of the river. Two sail factories are still in existence - one below Whitby School at the side of Bagdale Beck, now a furniture store, the other at Spital Bridge. I recall an old dry-dock partially filled with earth and rubble, it was situated on land now owned by Northern Electric. There are still areas where roperies are said to have been. (See map).

The Fishburns built three of Cook's ships but the 'Adventure' was built in Langbournes Yard. Commenting on the age of some wooden ships of those times, there is a record of a little schooner the 'Lively' ending her career on the Lincolnshire coast in 1885. She was built in Whitby and was more than a hundred years old. Which yard is not recorded; we can hardly say she came to an untimely end and it is also an indication of the manner in which some boats continued in use long after they should have been scrapped. This may be looked upon as further evidence of the sound construction of vessels made in local yards. It is also a revealing feature of how some ship owners were devoid of any humane consideration of the crew.

Other details give life and interest to what would otherwise be a monotonous list of ship names and yards where built. Numerous records in Customs papers, family papers, wills, costs of outlay when building a ship, could be included in here and

FOR
QUEBEC,
AND THE CANADAS,
With Goods & Passengers,
AND CARRIES A SURGEON:
THE FINE NEW SHIP
COLUMBUS,
BURTHEN 150 TONS,
H. BARRICK, COMMANDER;

WILL SAIL FROM WHITBY ABOUT THE FIRST WEEK IN

APRIL, 1832.

This Ship having a Poop and Forecastle, and 7ft 6in between Decks affords superior Accommodations for Passengers desirous to embark for America.

For Terms of Passage (the Ship finding Water and Fuel) and Freight of Goods, apply to Messrs H & G. BARRICK, Ship-Builders Whitby, who will give Letters of Recommendation to their Agent at Quebec; also, ample information respecting the employment of Labourers, and Small Capitalists for the Sale of Land in Upper Canada.

☞ Early applications are requested as the Ship is expected soon to be filled up.

R. RODGERS, PRINTER, WHITBY.

Gaskin was very meticulous in researching State papers with reference to Whitby affairs. Space precludes many of these details.

Whitby owners of sail craft were ready to take advantage of any charter which would offer a profitable settlement on completion of the undertaking.

The 'John Barry' (520 tonnage) was built in 1814 by the Barrys and was recorded as being employed (in 1835) transporting convicts, (260) to Australian penal settlements. Although London registered she was Whitby owned and launched from a yard between Boghall and where the railway station now stands.

There were also many emigrant ships sailing mainly to Quebec in Canada. The early 19th century was not a happy period for the British working classes and many took advantage of cheap land offers or employment across the Atlantic. The smallness of the emigrant ships and the lack of facilities must have made the voyages horrendous by our modern standards.

Between 1828 and 1834 several Whitby ships sailed direct to the St Lawrence carrying emigrants from the district. In 1828 the 'Crown' (383 tons) sailed with 30 passengers. The 'Addison' left in 1830 with 80 passengers but it would appear that the Barricks (my mother's family) seemed to have either 'packed them in' or to have been a popular or convenient choice for the crossing. The 'Gulnare' (338 tons) took 230, the 'Columbus' (467 tons) number of passengers not known, see bill advertising the voyage in 1832; the 'Hindoo' took 100 passengers in May 1832 and the 'Ida' also built in Henry Barrick's yard took emigrants in 1831.

Another ship the 'Majestic' built in H. and G. Barrick's yard and captained by another Henry Barrick sailed from Whitby in 1835 for Quebec, carrying mules, the ship was lost on passage up the River St. Lawrence at Brandy Pots, Hare Island. How many survived is not stated. It is interesting to note that the first steam paddle tug to be built in Whitby, the 'Streoneshalh' was built in H. and G. Barrick's yard in 1836 which was on the East side of the river in the area between the foot of Green Lane and the opening known as Boyes Staithe (commonly known as Abraham's Bosom). They built vessels there from 1828 to 1865.

In this era of sail, Whitby was certainly a centre of activity with the whaling vessels bringing in their catches for processing, the noise of hammering and banging of the various trades associated with the ship building industry, such as blacksmiths, joiners, caulkers, rope-makers, sail-makers, block and mast-makers and other related activities, swelling the general hubbub of the busy port.

On a piece of land where the gasworks once stood, (near the Viaduct) some of the large boiler houses were built within which the whale blubber was rendered down into oil. Everyone, I repeat, *everyone*, was frequently reminded of our whaling industry if the direction of the wind changed and the strong, filthy stench from the residue from the whale blubber was wafted round the town. The boiler houses might have been out of sight - they could not be out of mind. The residue, incidentally, was converted into manure.

The days of sail were drawing to an end with the invention of the steam engine. The Barricks built their last ship, a barque, the 'Victory' in 1865 but it was another barque the 'Monkshaven' (371 tons) built by Messrs. Smales Brothers and launched in 1871 that was to be the last of the sailing ships to be built in Whitby. Her career was short lived. Laden with 657 tons of coal she sailed for Valparaiso in 1876 but caught fire in the South Atlantic and was a total loss.

1837 was the year that the whale fishing from Whitby came to an end. Mineral oils were being introduced and the Government bounty was withdrawn. In that year

Above: Taking in sail in heavy weather. The four sailors on the foreyard are securing the mainsail to prevent it blowing away in the severe weather. A big wave has just broken over the starboard gunwale. The dangers of working aloft in these conditions are obvious.

Below: Steering in a heavy swell. The officer of the watch keeps an eye on the compass while two sailors look after the wheel. An extra hand was needed in these conditions to guard against the violent kicking of the rudder, which could cause serious injury to the helmsman.

two ships were being fitted for the Davis Straits - the 'Phoenix' (mentioned previously) and the 'Camden'. When the Phoenix sailed the weather was wild with thick snow showers blowing in from the North Sea. Despite the help of the tug, 'Streoneshalh' when crossing the bar, it was found impossible to hold her and she slewed round to starboard and was driven on to the Scar behind the East Pier. She lay there until the next spring tide and was then towed back into the harbour where she was found to be so badly damaged as to be unfit for whaling. The 'Camden' continued with her voyage but came back a *clean ship* (failed to make any catches) so that proved to be the demise of the industry here.

Incidentally, as the shipping trade of Whitby increased, (e.g. general trade, whale fishing, as remarked), an interesting phenomenon took place. The local youth of the town turned from fishing to manning the many sail vessels as there were better chances of improving their sea-going careers. There were many opportunities for lads to apprentice themselves and ultimately finish up as Master, (sometimes of their own ship). While Dr. Young was writing his history of Whitby in the early years of the 19th century he noted that in 1816 there were only nine fishermen but the number of seamen was 2674. Thus an employment pattern had been established in the 18th century which was to last through into the mid-20th century. Gaskin noted that then the main local fishing enterprises were carried on from Robin Hood's Bay, Staithes and Runswick. He wrote too, that in the early 20th century (at the time he wrote his history) the number of men fishing had risen to 150 but their usual craft was still the coble with a crew of three and still practising inshore fishing.

ROBIN HOOD'S BAY, STAITHES AND RUNSWICK
(Fishing centres during the Whaling period)

The 'Bay' as the above fishing town is known locally, certainly deserves the name Baytown as it is, even more so today, more like a small town than a fishing village. The fisherfolk were quick to take advantage of the increased fishing trade when many Whitby men chose to go whaling although doubtless men from the fishing villages would join the Whalers if they so wished.

The fishermen must have been a hardy breed as the job of launching their cobles in poor weather could be an exhausting task, let alone rowing off to the grounds where the fishing was to be done. There were many fatalities and an interesting but grim fact is worthy of note at this point. Staithes, Whitby, 'Bay' and Runswick fishermen more often than not wore a navy blue jersey (or guernsey), a closely knitted woollen garment. In each of the villages the women knitted their own distinctive pattern, recognised as being unique to that particular village. Thus should a body be washed ashore somewhere along the coastline - although the features might not be identifiable, a scrutiny of the pattern of his jersey would establish from which village he had set out. (The words jersey and guernsey appeared to have originated in the Channel Islands.)

The alum trade had been slowly declining and came to an end when the last alum works closed in 1850. Up till that time it had required many sloops or collier brigs for transport but the use of urine in the industry had been discontinued so that particular aspect of transport was no longer necessary.

A new name appeared among Whitby ship owners in the early 19th century that of the Turnbulls who recorded numerous transactions related to the supplying of the alum trade with sea-borne commodities of one sort or another.

Robin Hood's Bay in two moods

In 1835 a new swivel bridge had replaced Whitby's old drawbridge giving a clearance of 45ft 3ins to vessels proceeding from the inner harbour and out to sea. This clearance proved to be an important factor in later ship building but not one to the advantage of the industry as might be supposed.

The large number of seamen in Whitby, let alone the numerous tradesmen connected with ship-building, was a clear indication the port was a town whose very mainstay was the sea - at any rate in the first half of the 19th century. At that time not very much thought was being given to ship propulsion other than the customary use of wind power but a new power was being experimented with, even at the end of the 18th century. A Patrick Miller had tried out various types of paddle ships powered by gangs of men - the principal result of these experiments was the collapse of all the men. He did however, turn to steam and the end result was the 'Comet' built by Robertson of Glasgow in 1812. It is sufficient to say that the efforts to utilize steam power in water transport were significantly successful in the 19th century. The application of steam to shipping was swift from a general usage point of view but even into the 20th century sail vessels continued in use in some of the more technically advanced nations as well as the poorer countries. The 'Comet' brought the realization that such a vessel would have its limitations but would be valuable as a tug. That proved to be the case when the first steam paddle tug to be built in Whitby towed the 'Phoenix' over the harbour bar. The tug although built in Whitby had to be towed to Sunderland on completion to have an engine fitted as nowhere else in the port had any yard developed the technical aspects of constructing a complicated marine engine.

The fortunes of the Turnbulls prospered and no doubt the family would discuss ways and means of further advances to their enterprises as their initial purchase of a sloop, the 'Yarm', had been augmented to a small fleet of sloops, mainly in the 1830's and establishing them as shipowners.

Possibly with ship building in mind, Thomas Turnbull, whose son was also named Thomas had him apprenticed to Henry Barrick in 1835 who, at that time, had the biggest ship-yard in Whitby (census 1851). Here he received a sound instruction in the art of practical and theoretical ship building.

It was said that the young Thomas was very interested in the new phenomenon of steam navigation and was fortunate in being able to follow the construction of the 'Streoneshalh' in a neighbouring Barrick yard (George & Henry Barrick).

Finally the Turnbulls decided to enter the ship-building trade and rented the Larpool Yard in 1840. Sail vessels were still in demand and it was in that sphere that they built their first craft - two brigs, around 240 tons each and a schooner of 80 tons. Three more vessels were built but after that it was considered a wise move to close the yard as the economic climate was far from favourable.

The 1840's generally known as the 'Hungry Forties' proved to be a slump period and the country suffered from a recession in many industries. The decision to close down at Larpool had been a wise one but the Turnbulls in 1843 then rented a small yard situated at Boghall which had dry-dock facilities and carried out repairs on their small fleet of sail craft and also the requirements of some other ship-owners.

IRON AND STEAM

The recovery from the slump had started around 1845 - in 1850 a period of prosperity then commenced and in many areas of industry there was a rapid expansion, in particular, in the construction of tramp ships in the latter part of the 19th century.

RUNSWICK BAY *(Northern area)*

Painting by John Slater (Published by courtsey of the Gatehouse Collection, Robin Hood's Bay)

The village lies at the foot of towering cliffs. As at Robin Hood's Bay, the quaint cottages are connected by narrrow alleys and flights of steps. In 1666 a landslip destroyed the whole village but no lives were lost. In 1816 the villagers were said to have manned 40 cobles - again it was during the whaling era.

STAITHES

Painting by John Slater (Published by courtesy of The Gatehouse Collection, Robin Hoods Bay

Staithes originally a Scandinavian settlement was said to have had over 400 fishermen using the small harbour - probably during the whaling period. The famous James Cook lived here for a time before starting his sea career.

Foreign trade was bringing much greater awards than had been possible in the coastal trade and it was with this knowledge in mind that local businessmen, ship-owners plus non-seagoing, but moneyed persons contemplated a change in financial tactics - that of investing in tramp ship companies.

Reverting to Turnbulls - Thomas, the younger, became very much aware of the potentialities of steam after his experience with the 'Streoneshalh's' construction.

Most other local ship-owners had been inclined to deride it and considered the strange production that came out of the Barrick yard, with its long thin funnel and its large thrashing paddle wheels as the work of cranks. Thomas and his father had the gift of perceiving that indeed, this new power would see the end of sail and the thoughts of them both were now concerned with the pros and cons of constructing iron ships which would use the new motive power.

They decided to buy the Whitehall Yard, down the river from Larpool Yard, which had better facilities and was almost opposite the smaller Boghall Yard. What convinced them they had made the right decision was hearing that in 1852 the 'John Bowes', Tyne built and fitted with a screw propellor had made a passage to London from Newcastle with a full cargo of coal and was back again in the Tyne within 5 days.

As far as Whitby was concerned the 'Streoneshalh' and the 'John Bowes' were sign-posts pointing the way to a new era in shipping and men with acumen and sound judgement were not slow to appreciate what was needed.

At the Whitehall Yard the Turnbulls, between 1852 and 1870 had built many sailing ships as there was still a demand for these vessels in that period. However, steam power applied to shipping was developing quickly and in 1870 the yard com-

This old photo of Swansea Harbour in 1843 shows two steam paddle-boats which suggest that the early steam paddle-tug built in Whitby with its long, thin funnel and large thrashing paddle wheels was in fact no different from the many paddle-tugs of that period. Photograph by courtesy of the National Maritime Museum, Greenwich.

menced building iron steam ships. Between 1871 and 1902 the Turnbull Yard turned out 118 steamships, many for Turnbull companies but others were ordered from elsewhere.

The Turnbulls were a large family and space does not permit a full explanation of the various shipping concerns in which they participated other than naming their main shipping company below.

A new phase in shipping began - that of the tramp ships and once again names of steamship companies became as well known as the sail-ship builders of the 18th and early 19th century.

The First Whitby companies of any prominence and which were to remain so until the mid-20th century were the Turnbull (and later Turnbull & Scott S.S. Co.) and the Rowland & Marwood S.S. Co., (later some of their ships were managed by W. Headlam & Son. There were other local companies with smaller fleets - Pymans, Harrowings, Smales & Barrys.

The Turnbulls having acquired the Whitehall Yard (and the mansion above it of the same name) set about converting the dock yard with the intention of building their first iron ship. New equipment was needed and considerable expense was involved, but the keel of the first iron ship was laid in February 1871, just over a hundred years ago, and was completed and launched in June of that year. The launch was watched by hundreds, those lining Esk Terrace, Low Road and Boghall areas having the best views.

PADDLE-STEAM TUGS IN WHITBY HARBOUR - LATE 19th CENTURY

Early steam tugs were invaluable in the 19th century in all ports of importance (Whitby was the 7th most important in England, 8th in the UK) and as demonstrated, supplanted the old methods of a well-manned coble towing out the sail-ships or heaving themselves out via the capstans on the West Pier, once their ropes were attached. The tugs shown in the Sutcliffe photograph were busier still when the Turnbulls launched their iron ships, not only pulling them out of the harbour but up to Sunderland for the fitting of their marine engines.

In 1872 Reginald M. Turnbull and a cousin, Robert Turnbull Scott, registered themselves into Joint partnership and the Turnbull & Scott S.S. Co., came into being. The Dockyard and shipping company which then existed were managed through the family.

In 1880 the family had sold all its sail vessels and concentrated on building iron (later) steel ships to augment their fleet as well as fulfilling orders. In the first ten years following the Yard's foundation, fifty-two ships were built, twenty-five of which were to become part of the Turnbull & Son Fleet. Other ships were built for well known companies, Hogarths, Pyman as well as for many smaller companies.

Whitby Bridge (mentioned previously) was to be the cause, together with a slump, of the closure of Whitehall Dock Yard. Bigger ships were now easier to build and a wider beam (width) enabling them to carry more cargo was required. The narrow channel through the bridge did not allow a wider ship to pass so the yard closed in 1902 and never again was ship construction to be of such importance to the town.

Yet another local tramp ship company of some importance was the Rowland & Marwood company which was incorporated in 1890 - the names of some shareholders & ships together with the number of shares held are given below (more from an interest point of view). Nearly all their ships were built in Sunderland and used steam power indicating that both Turnbull & Scott and Rowland & Marwood were going 'full steam ahead'.

In 1901 two Rowland & Marwood ships found themselves contending with a vicious hurricane in the Gulf of Mexico. One, the S.S. Roma was said to have been washed so far inland on the Mexican coast that all efforts to refloat her failed. The last that was heard of her was that she was substituting as 'a ready built hotel'.

Whitby Gazette

Friday 7 August 1891

THE WHITEHALL SHIP-YARD - We learn that it is the intention of Messrs. Thomas Turnbull and Son shortly to lay down the stocks for a large steamer for their own account. For some months now the yard has been very quiet, and it is cause for thankfulness that employment will be given in the course of a month or two to several of the old hands connected with the yard who have been but partially employed either at Whitby or elsewhere for some considerable time. Of course, the building of one steamer will not put the yard in anything like its former state of activity, but with the resumption of building operations there is always a hope that more contracts will follow, and thus utilize willing and capable hands in the production of local and national wealth.

The two companies gave their ships names with a local connection - Turnbull & Scott using Whitby street names or other well-known locations terminating in 'gate' (e.g. Baxtergate, Sandgate, Redgate etc) The Rowland & Marwood ships were named after local villages (e.g. Sneaton, Goathland, Glaisdale) their last ship the Egton being a fine vessel as too was the 'Runswick' of 1956 (see photos below).

The Depression years of the thirties were especially bad for shipping and many owners had to lay up their ships. The Second World War did inject 'new life' into the local companies (if that is an appropriate expression to use considering the number that were torpedoed) and there were many ships soon operating on Government Service for one reason or another.

Both local tramp-ship companies ceased their activities in the latter part of the 20th century as foreign competition was fierce and under-cutting was easily accomplished in a variety of ways. The Egton, after several years lying idle in Hartlepool Dock was sold for scrap to a Finnish company, although she was only built in 1962.

Shareholders of R.& M. S.S.Co.

THE SCHEDULE ABOVE REFERRED TO.

Signatures of Vendors.	Steam Ships.	No. of Shares.	Price.	Signatures of Witnesses to Signatures of Vendors.
J. BELLERBY...	Resolution.	1	At the rate of £450 for each sixty - fourth share.	George Buchannan
WM. WRIGHT	Resolution.	10	At the rate of £450 for each sixty - fourth share.	George Buchannan
JAS. S. MOSS...	Resolution.	3	At the rate of £450 for each sixty - fourth share.	George Buchannan
JOHN ROWLAND CHRISR. MARWOOD ... }	Resolution.	7	At the rate of £450 for each sixty - fourth share.	George Buchannan
J. BELLERBY...	Discovery.	1	At the rate of £450 for each sixty - fourth share.	George Buchannan
WM. WRIGHT	Discovery.	11	At the rate of £450 for each sixty - fourth share.	George Buchannan
JAS. S. MOSS...	Discovery.	3	At the rate of £450 for each sixty - fourth share.	George Buchannan
JOHN ROWLAND CHRISR. MARWOOD ... }	Discovery.	6	At the rate of £450 for each sixty - fourth share.	George Buchannan
WM. WRIGHT	Enterprise.	13	At the rate of £450 for each sixty - fourth share.	George Buchannan
JAS. S. MOSS...	Enterprise.	1	At the rate of £450 for each sixty - fourth share.	George Buchannan

R & M Steam-ship Co Ltd Whitby
COMPANY'S FLEET.

	Built.	Deadweight Tons (approx.)
S.S. " SCORESBY "	January, 1923	6,750
S.S. " KILDALE "	April, 1924	6,850
S.S. " GOATHLAND "	April, 1924	6,830
S.S. " FYLINGDALE "	December, 1924	6,760
S.S. " LARPOOL "	December, 1924	6,850
S.S. " SNEATON "	March, 1925	5,900
S.S. " SANDSEND "	June, 1925	5,950
S.S. " STREONSHALH "	July, 1928	6,100
S.S. " SALTWICK "	November, 1929	6,550
S.S. " RUNSWICK "	May, 1930	6,770
S.S. " STAKESBY "	June, 1930	6,860

72,470

at July 1931.

The decline of the Merchant Service was a blow to Whitby and Robin Hood's Bay and other local men who had found employment in the local companies. The closure of the Whitehall Yard also caused the loss of 800 jobs and although many men turned to the local shipping companies the loss of employment through the ensuing decline meant that Whitby's importance as a well known port faded into the past.

Nevertheless, as in times long ago, the fishing industry continues. Today (verified in March 1991) there are still around 150 fishermen; 85 employed in keel boats and 65 in cobles. All cobles now have engines and the once familiar sails have vanished. The keel boats which began to replace the 'Mules' in the 1940's are equipped with modern technology and doubtless save on man power - the important factor now is the control of the fast disappearing fish stocks which provide a livelihood. Our once prolific fishing areas have been plundered by craft from elsewhere which, at times, fished irresponsibly and illegally - and still do if we can believe reported incidents.

Formerly there were always the feverish annual seasons of herring fishing, in particular, before the First World War and again in the years immediately following the Second. The Whitby Gazette report of August 1891 demonstrates that fleets from Cornwall came up annually too.

I well remember in the late Forties the fleets of fishing boats, many of them Scottish ones, which followed the huge herring shoals down the North Sea. It was no exaggeration to state that it was possible to walk across the lower harbour at Whitby via the crowded fishing vessels which berthed there with their catches. When they left harbour at night, it was the custom for hundreds of people to assemble on the piers to watch them cast off and make their way out to the harbour mouth. In the dusk it was as though a city had miraculously appeared in the sea as hundreds of lights flickered and bobbed as they headed for the Dogger Bank and other fishing areas.

Taken about 1950 - Kirkwall boats and Whitby Mules during the herring season.

My father talked of the hundreds of Scots fisher lasses - pre First World War who travelled down from the Northern Scottish ports and worked long hours on the quays, gutting and preparing the herring for packing with salt, into small wooden barrels for onward shipment to Danish, German and other continental ports.

To this very day the Dutch still treat as a delicacy, the raw herring which they eat with relish.

Having said that, I would not be completing this review if I did not mention Bernard McCall's useful analysis of local trade developments in his book 'Whitby - Modern Sea Port'. I recall that between the two World Wars the only ship of significant tonnage to enter the harbour, other than fishing boats, but still of what one could call the coaster class, was the yearly arrival of a timber ship which unloaded its cargo at the Eskside Wharf.

Since 1955 Mr McCall has kept a detailed account of ships and cargoes - both exports and imports - and although the trade has fluctuated , nevertheless it has renewed Whitby's involvement with sea trade - not however, one which involves many local men, nor local ship-building. Whether or not this trade will grow with the opening of a Common Market is a matter for the future.

I dislike to finish on a somewhat pessimistic note but, having firmly placed Whitby as a port noted for its important role in shipping history, one can only deplore the

29

Rowland and Marwood S.S. Company Flag

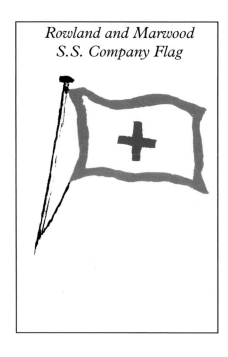

fact that our once renowned fleet of merchant ships has now vanished.

Past generations of seamen assisted in building a country whose language today is internationally spoken, whose influence is still considerable but which one day may regret the abandonment of its Merchant Marine.

An interesting fact, probably not now widely known, was that originally the Rowland & Marwood S.S. Company's flag was a red cross on a white background. This was changed to a blue cross on a white background on smoke stacks as depicted here, as a result of an official request for the Company to so comply, the reason being that it was normal international practice to designate hospital ships and, indeed, hospital bases ashore, with that well-known insignia. This change, I understand, was made in the early thirties.

S.S. SARMATIA

Built in 1889 at Sunderland by W. Doxford & Sons. Owned by a Whitby company known as 'International Line S.S. Co. Ltd.'. Managed by Christopher Marwood who was founder of the Rowland & Marwood S.S. Co. Ltd. Sold to Rowland & Marwood S.S. Co. Ltd in 1901 then to an Italian company, in 1906 - renamed 'AUDAX'. 27 October 1916 sailed from Glasgow bound for Genoa and thereafter disappeared. Last reported on 30th October 1916 (Lloyds).

S.S. SCORESBY built Jan 1923

S.S.GOATHLAND built Dec 1924

S.S. LARPOOL built Dec 1924

S.S. RUNSWICK built May 1930

S.S. STAKESBY built June 1930

S.S. Larpool on passage either in the Baltic or the St. Lawrence river. Both were closed in winter in pre-2nd World War days. Autumn 1937

M.V. RUNSWICK built 1956

M.V. EGTON in Liverpool

The M.S. Egton at Liverpool - the last of the Rowland & Headlam Shipping Line - one of the many victims of the decline of the British Merchant Navy in the latter part of the 20th century.

She left Hartlepool on 6th January 1986, in a snow storm. Her sudden departure was evidently something of a surprise to those who were interested in her fate.

Towed by the tug 'Formidable' of the Alexander Towing Co., she eventually arrived at a small Finnish port on the 18th January 1986. Whether she was actually broken up or re-sold is not certain but her departure marked the closure of an era in Whitby's history.

Report in the Whitby Gazette:- Egton's final voyage

The cargo vessel Egton (14800 tons) which has been in 'mothballs' in Jackson Dock, Hartlepool, for the last seven years, was due to begin her final voyage this morning. The ship, the last on the books of Rowland & Marwood, and formerly managed by Headlam & Sons, the old established shipping concern with headquarters at Raithwaite, near Whitby, was expected to be towed out on the morning's tide. Her destination is Helsinki. She was sold to a Finnish buyer last Friday.

m.s. "EGTON".		by	BARTRAM & SONS LTD., SUNDERLAND.		
Built 1962			To the order of		
			HEADLAM & SON, WHITBY.		
Dimensions.			**Tonnages.**		
				Shelter Deck.	
Length overall	507' 7"			Open.	Closed
" B.P.	475' 0½"				
Breadth extreme	66' 1¾"		Gross	7,175	9,958
Depth moulded	31' 6" - 2nd Deck.		Nett	3,939	5,698
	41' 0" - Upper Deck.		Deadweight	12,500	14,831
			Draft	27' 4"	30' 7"

Engines built by
WILLIAM DOXFORD & SONS (ENGINEERS) LTD.
SUNDERLAND.

Doxford "P" Type, Opposed Piston, Turbo charged. 6,640 B.H.P.

Two ship photos from the G. Spark Collection of 80 plus coasting vessels which have docked in Whitby in the last few years. Some were of foreign origin but the majority were British.

The 'Boisterence' (reg. Rochester) a weekly visitor with a steel cargo. First arrived in Whitby on 15th Oct 1984.

The "Island Dart" (reg. Rochester) previously named "Gardience" unloading soya at Endeavour Wharf.

COMPANY FLAG

S.S. Parracombe' - formerly a Pyman ship. Torpedoed in mid-Atlantic 4 April 1941.
'S.S. Welcombe' sister ship - bombed and sunk by Heinkel aircraft on unescorted voyage to
Malta same month.

ACKNOWLEDGEMENTS

I wish to acknowledge the help given by the following persons - Captain
N. Jameson whose advice was always available, Mr. G. Spark who supplied me with
the two photographs of the modern coasters, Mr. D. Davidson for providing yet
more photos of ships belonging to the Rowland & Marwood Fleet and
Mr. P. Hansell for the up-to-date details of our present fishing fleet. My thanks to
John Dixon (Preston) who supplied the facts on the S.S. Sarmatia and to Mr. John
Tindale who allowed me the use of the 1778 map of Whitby. I am grateful also to
Mr. W. Eglon Shaw whose Sutcliffe photographs add value to the text, Mr. John
Freeman for the use of his drawing of Whitby Harbour Entrance and Messrs.
Fielding for use of the two paintings of Staithes and Runswick Bay (Gatehouse
Collection, Robin Hood's Bay). Mr. Bill Robertson and Mr. Angus McBride who
acceded to my request to include their drawings of whaling ships and Mr. David
Marcombe whose photos of life on the whalers demonstrate clearly the dangers, also
the help of the staff of Whitby Library.

I wish to mention again Mr. T. Turnbull who agreed to my use of the private edition
of his family's history and to acknowledge the help and advice given by Major Jim
Milton who also read through the original manuscript.

Finally, a belated acknowledgement to Mrs. Cordelia Stamp whose helpful advice
influenced and assisted in the publishing sphere both the publication of 'The Red
Duster' and the booklet 'Home Port'